Christ Is God's Middle Name

Books by Edward S. Fox

Hunger Valley
Massacre Inlet

Illustrated by Ursula Landshoff

Christ Is God's Middle Name

Children Talk About God

Edward S. and Elizabeth H. Fox

Doubleday & Company, Inc., Garden City, New York
1971

Preface

This book had its beginning in the statement made by a five-year-old that God is a millionaire because in church grownups give Him dollars; but that Jesus is poor because in Sunday school the children give *Him* only pennies. It was such a naïve and startling remark that we continued the conversation, discussing God, and Jesus, and Heaven, and some of the better-known Bible stories read to children either at home or in Sunday school. We came away from this first talk intrigued by our little five-year-old's earnest faith and considerable confusion about Christian beliefs. So intrigued were we that, later, we sat down to compare our own early thoughts on religion, and were no less intrigued to discover that we had been equally as naïve and equally as confused as our five-year-old. This prompted more talks with other children (ages five through seven) and out of them grew a new area of interest to us: children's vulnerability to their fears, hopes, and lack of security, as well as to their relationship with other people, parents, brothers and sisters, friends, strangers. Many of the talks were either too stereotyped or too repetitive to present; and the ones chosen are not verbatim, an impossibility the way some children ramble on, while others are too reticent. The subject of God was the doorway that led us, inadvertently at first, then purposely, into the inner recesses of young minds. The researching and the writing of this book have been an experience, sometimes amusing, sometimes sad. Above all else, the one thing we learned was that to most children God, though mystifying, is very real and very important, far more than we had realized until we had entered, and shared, their world, even for a short time.

Edward S. and Elizabeth H. Fox

Christ Is God's Middle Name

David

"Who's God, David?"

"God."

"Can you tell me a little more about who He is?"

"God's just God."

"Can you tell me what He's like?"

"Yes."

"What?"

"He's a man."

"What sort of a man?"

"A big man."

"How big?"

"Big as the whole world."

"Have you ever seen Him?"

"No."

"Then how do you know He's big?"

"My mother says so."

"What does your mother say?"

"That God's everywhere."

"So if God's everywhere He must be big?"

"Yes."

"Has your mother ever seen Him?"

"She can't."

"Why can't she?"

"He's a magician."

"In what way is He a magician?"

"He's invisible."

"All of the time? Or some of the time?"

"All of the time."

"Do you know why He's invisible all of the time?"

Silence.

"Where does God live, David?"

"In the sky."

"Where in the sky?"

"Up high."

"How high up?"

"Way up."

"Does He live in a house or something?"

"Yes."

"What?"

"A castle."

"Does He live alone?"

"No."

"Who lives with Him?"

"Angels."

"What're angels?"

"People with wings."

"You mean they can fly?"

"Yes."

"Have you ever seen any angels?"

"Nobody can."

"Why can't they?"

"They're invisible, too."

"Would you like to see an angel, David?"

"No."

"Would you like to see God?"

"No."

"Why wouldn't you?"

"Because only people who die see God and angels. And I don't want to die."

Sandra

"Who's God, Sandra?"

"My shepherd."

"Do you know what a shepherd is?"

"He takes care of sheep."

"But you're not a sheep."

"God's a special kind of shepherd."

"In what way?"

"He takes care of me."

"How do you know?"

"It says so in the psalm."

"What does the psalm say?"

" 'The Lord is my shepherd and I shall not want.' "

"What is meant by 'I shall not want'?"

"Not having things."

"What sort of things?"

"A house, and clothes, and food, and a car, and a television set."

"Don't you have all of those?"

"Yes."

"And you don't ever worry about not having them?"

"No, but—"

"But what?"

"My father and mother do."

"How do you know that?"

"They're always fighting and arguing."

"About what?"

"Money."

"In what way?"

"My father says everything costs so much these days there isn't enough to go around, and if my mother doesn't stop spending more than he makes they'll lose everything."

"You're worried about your father and mother, aren't you, Sandra?"

"Yes."

"Why?"

"I hate to hear them argue, especially when they don't have to."

"They don't have to?"

"Not if they believed in my shepherd."

"He isn't just *your* shepherd?"

"He's mine, and everybody's, if only they would let Him be."

"Won't your father and mother let Him be?"

"No."

"Why won't they?"

"They're too busy with other things."

Joe

"Who's God, Joe?"
"The man in Heaven I pray to."
"When do you pray to Him, Joe?"
"Every night before I go to bed."
"What kind of prayers do you say?"
"The usual ones."
"What others?"
"I ask for things."
"What sort of things?"
"Right now I'm praying for a new bike."
"What else are you asking for?"
"Strength."
"What kind of strength?"
"Muscles."
"Why muscles?"
"So I can beat up Chick Lowry."
"Who's Chick Lowry?"
"The bully in our grade."
"Do you think God will answer your prayers, Joe?"
"I know He will."
"Why are you so positive?"
"After the one a couple of weeks ago I just am."

"What prayer did He answer a couple of weeks ago?"

"My mother got sick and almost died."

"Almost?"

"She's okay now."

"And you prayed for her, of course."

"Harder than I've ever prayed before."

"And it was your prayers that made her well again?"

"Yes."

"How do you know?"

"What else could have?"

Bobby

"Who's God, Bobby?"

"I dunno."

"You haven't any idea?"

"Nope."

"Do you know what God's like?"

"Nope."

"Is He a man?"

"I dunno."

"Where does He live?"

"I dunno."

"What do you know about Him?"

"Nothin' much."

"Do you go to Sunday school, Bobby?"

"Nope."

"Church?"

"Nope."

"Do your father and mother go to church?"

"Nope."

"You've heard of God, haven't you?"

"Sure."

"Where?"

"School."

"Your teacher talks about Him at school?"

"Nope."

"Who does?"

"Some of the kids."

"What do they say?"

"Goddamn it."

"What else?"

"Goddamn you."

"Why?"

"They're mad."

"Don't they know they're swearing?"

"Sure."

"And isn't swearing wrong?"

"Sure."

"Why're you sure?"

"Because the teacher punishes them when she catches them."

"Who else do you hear talking about God?"

"My father."

"What does your father say?"

"Goddamn it."

"When?"

"When he's mad."

"What else does he say?"

"Goddamn you."

"When does he say that?"

"When he's mad at my mother."

"What does your mother say?"

"Nothing."

"Does it upset her?"

"Yes."

"What does she do?"

"Cries."

Pete

"Who's God, Pete?"

"He's against the Devil."

"In what way is God against the Devil?"

"God is good."

"And the Devil?"

"The Devil's bad."

"Then they mustn't get on too well together."

"They fight all the time."

"Where?"

"In people."

"Do they ever fight in you, Pete?"

"Yes."

"How do you know?"

"I can feel it."

"How can you feel it?"

"I get all uptight."

Linda

"Who's God, Linda?"

"A king."

"What kind of a king?"

"Just a king."

"What's He king of?"

"The world."

"What's He like, Linda?"

"You mean, what does He look like?"

"That. And is He a good king or a bad king?"

"He's a good king."

"How do you know He's a good king?"

"Because He loves everyone."

"How do you know that?"

"It says so in the book our teacher reads to us in Sunday school. My mother and father say so, too."

"And you know what He looks like?"

"Yes."

"Will you tell me?"

"He looks like a hippie."

"How does He look like a hippie?"

"He has whiskers."

"What kind of whiskers?"

"Long ones all over his face. And He has long hair."

"What else?"

"He wears dresses."

"Like your mother's?"

"No. My mother wears minis, and His go all the way down to the ground."

"Like a robe?"

"Sort of."

"Do you think a king should look like a hippie?"

"I guess so."

"How do you know He looks like one?"

"From pictures."

"Then you've never seen God?"

"Of course not."

"Why not?"

"Because He's dead."

"God's dead?"

"Yes."

"When did He die?"

"A long time ago."

"Do you know how He died?"

"Sure."

"How?"

"On a cross."

"A cross?"

"Sure."

"Did you ever hear of Jesus, Linda?"

"Of course."

"Who is He?"

"God."

"Jesus is God?"

"Sure."

"They're both the same?"

"Sure."

"Why're you so sure?"

"Jesus is God's first name."

"Did you ever hear of Christ, Linda?"

"That's God's middle name."

"Then his full name is Jesus Christ God."

"Yes."

"One thing puzzles me, Linda. How can God be king of the whole world if He's dead?"

"He isn't really dead."

"In what way isn't He really dead?"

"He *was* dead, but He came alive again."

"How did that happen?"

"He went to Heaven."

"Everyone who dies comes alive again in Heaven?"

"Yes."

"And God rules the world from Heaven?"

"Yes."

"How?"

"He has helpers."

"What kind of helpers?"

"They're called disciples."

"How many disciples does He have, Linda?"

"Hundreds. Thousands."

"Can you name one?"

"Of course."

"Who?"

"Mr. Appleton."

"Who's Mr. Appleton?"

"The minister in our church."

Ned

"Who's God, Ned?"
"He tells me things I should and shouldn't do."
"What things?"
"I can't remember them all."
"What ones do you remember?"
"I should love Him."
"What else?"
"I should honor my father and my mother."
"What else?"
"I shouldn't kill anything."
"Go on."
"I shouldn't steal."
"Go on."
"I should go to church on Sunday."
"Are there any more?"
"Yes."
"Do you obey God in all of them?"
"I'm not sure."
"Why aren't you sure?"
"What's adultery?"

Alice

"Who's God, Alice?"

"Noah's friend."

"Do you mean Noah who built the Ark?"

"Yes."

"How do you know that God and Noah were friends?"

"It says in the Bible."

"What does the Bible say?"

"That God saved Noah's life."

"From the Flood?"

"Yes."

"Why did God send the Flood, Alice?"

"Because the world was full of bad people and He wanted them dead."

"Did God save anybody but Noah?"

"Yes."

"Who?"

"Mrs. Noah."

"Anybody else?"

"Noah's sons and their wives."

"Who else?"

"Two of every kind of animal and bird and snake and fish and bug."

"And when the Flood was over the world was a good place to live in?"

"For a while, I guess."

"Don't you think it's a good place now?"

"No."

"Why not?"

"It's full of bad people again."

"Why do you think that?"

"I hear my mother and father talking about them, and I see them on television."

"Do they frighten you?"

"Yes."

"Why, Alice?"

"Because God might send another flood."

Eddie

"Who's God, Eddie?"

"My Father."

"Your Father?"

"Yes."

"What's He like, Eddie?"

Silence.

"Would you rather not talk about Him?"

"Sure."

"Will you tell me then?"

"I don't know how."

"Why don't you know how?"

"Because I've never seen Him."

"Then you don't really know what He's like?"

"Of course I do."

"You mean, you just don't know what He *looks* like."

"Yes."

"But you do know what He's like in other ways?"

"Yes."

"Will you tell me what He's like in other ways?"

"I can talk to Him."

"You can?"

"Yes."

"What about?"

"Things."

"What sort of things?"

"Everything."

"Will you tell me some of the things you can talk to Him about?"

"He helps me in my schoolwork."

"Helps you how?"

"When I don't know the answer to a question I ask Him."

"And He tells it to you?"

"No."

"Why doesn't He?"

"I can talk to Him, but He can't talk to *me*."

"Then how does He give you the answer?"

"He puts it into my head."

"What else do you talk to Him about?"

"Troubles."

"Do you have many troubles?"

"Yes."

"And when you tell Him about them what happens?"

"They don't seem so bad."

"What else does your Father do for you, Eddie?"

"He brings food."

"What else?"

"He doesn't let me die when I'm asleep."

"Your Father must spend a lot of time with you."

"Yes."

"You must feel very close to Him and love Him very much."

"Yes."

"And He must love *you* very much."

"I think so."

"You're a lucky boy to have two fathers to love you and help you."

"I don't have two fathers to love me and help me."

"You don't?"

"No."

"Will you tell me why you don't have two fathers to love and help you, Eddie?"

"My other father can't."

"Can't?"

"No."

"Why can't he?"

"He doesn't live at home any more with my mother and me."

"Where does he live, Eddie?"

"With another lady."

Jane

"Who's God, Jane?"
"A bad man."
"A what?"
"A bad man."
"Why do you say He's bad?"
"Because He is."
"Why is He?"
"He just is."
"In what way?"
"He's mean."
"How is He mean?"
"He does mean things."
"What sort of mean things?"
"Lots of things."
"What, for instance?"
"He makes people sick."
"What else?"
"He makes people die."
"What else?"
"He makes people hate each other."
"Hate how?"
"They fight."
"Who fights?"

"Everybody in the world."

"Do you think the world is a bad place, Jane?"

"Yes."

"And God's bad for making it the way it is?"

"Yes."

"Are you sure that God makes all these things happen, Jane?"

"Of course."

"We've talked only about the bad things that God makes happen, Jane. What about the good things?"

"What good things?"

"The sun, and the moon, and the stars. Don't you think they're good things?"

"I guess so."

"And what about the animals and the birds, and the trees and the flowers?"

"I guess so."

"And what about the knowledge He's given man; in medicine, and inventions, like cars, and airplanes, and boats, and all the thousands of things we use in our everyday lives?"

"I guess."

"And most of all, Jane, what about God's bringing children into the world? Isn't that a good thing?"

Silence.

"What is it, Jane? Why are you crying?"

Silence.

"Please, Jane. Tell me why you're crying."

"I wish I hadn't ever been brought into the world."

"You what?"

"I wish I hadn't ever been brought into the world."

"Why do you wish that?"

Silence.

"Jane, don't you think you should tell me now the real reason you think God is bad and mean?"

"He made me ugly."

"Who says you're ugly?"

"The kids at school."

"Why?"

"Because my teeth stick out."

"What do they say?"

"They call me Bugs Bunny."

"You shouldn't let what a few kids at school say get you down."

"They aren't the only ones."

"Who else says things?"

"My father."

"How do you know?"

"I heard him fighting with my mother."

"What about?"

"Me."

"What about you?"

"He said I was ugly."

"He used the word 'ugly'?"

"Yes."

"What did he say?"

"I was an ugly duckling."

"What did your mother say?"

"That when I grew older my teeth could be fixed."

"Didn't you father agree?"

"No."

"Why didn't he?"

"He said it would cost too much and wouldn't make me look any better anyway."

"What did your mother say to that?"

"Nothing."

"Have you ever asked God for help, Jane?"

"I used to."

"Why did you stop?"

"He wouldn't do anything."

"Don't you think He likes you?"

"No."

"And your father and mother?"

"No."

"And the kids in school?"

"No."

"I'm sorry you feel this way, Jane."

Silence.

"Please, Jane. Please, don't cry."

Billy

"Who's God, Billy?"

"Clouds."

"Clouds?"

"Yes."

"What kind of clouds?"

"The big ones like castles."

"They're God?"

"Not the clouds themselves."

"What are?"

"The faces."

"The faces you see in the clouds?"

"Yes."

"And each one you see is God?"

"Yes."

"That makes quite a lot of Gods, doesn't it, Billy?"

"No."

"No?"

"It's the same God. He just makes different faces."

"How many different kinds of faces does He make?"

"Hundreds."

"Which do you like best?"

"The smiley ones."

"Why the smiley ones?"

"They mean He's happy."

"What other ones do you like?"

"The funny ones."

"Why?"

"They mean He's happy, too."

"Are there any you don't like?"

"Yes."

"Which are they?"

"The scowly ones."

"Why don't you like them?"

"They're scary."

"Why're they scary?"

"They mean He's mad."

"At whom?"

"I don't know."

"How did you learn that the faces in the clouds are God, Billy?"

"From Charley."

"Who's Charley?"

"My friend."

"A friend in your school?"

"No."

"In another school?"

"No."

"Is he a neighbor?"

"Sort of."

"Where does he live?"

"Down by Oak Creek."

"I don't know of any houses down by Oak Creek."

"He lives on a boat."

"I don't know of any boats in Oak Creek, either."

"It isn't in the creek."

"Where is it?"

"On dry land. In the weeds."

"How old is your friend Charley, Billy?"

"A hundred."

"A hundred?"

"He says he is."

"He must be poor if he's living in an abandoned boat."

"He's a millionaire."

"How do you know?"

"He says he is."

"Do you get to see him very often?"

"Every Saturday."

"Why?"

"I like to."

"What do you do when you go to see him?"

"Fish."

"What else?"

"Talk."

"What about?"

"Things."

"What things?"

"Everything."

"Does he know about everything?"

"Yes."

"He must be very smart."

"He's the smartest man in the world."

"Tell me, Billy. Did you ever talk to your father about God?"

"Once."

"What did he say?"

"To ask my mother."

"What did your mother say?"

"To ask my teacher."

"Did you ask your teacher?"

"Yes."

"What did she say?"

"She wanted me to go to the Sunday school where she teaches, too."

"And did you?"

"No."

"You wouldn't like to go to her Sunday school and learn more about God?"

"No."

"Why wouldn't you?"

"I don't have to now."

"Why don't you have to now?"

"Because I've already learned all about God from my friend, Charley."

Pam

"Who's God, Pam?"

"He gives parties."

"Where?"

"In His house."

"In what way are they parties, Pam?"

"Everybody gets dressed up in their best clothes."

"In what other way are they parties?"

"There're flowers everywhere."

"How else?"

"Everybody sings and is happy."

"Does God give these parties every Sunday, Pam?"

"No."

"They're special parties?"

"Oh, yes."

"When are they?"

"On Jesus' birthday."

"When else?"

"When Jesus went to Heaven."

"Why is it that everybody is so happy on these days, Pam?"

"Because they love Jesus."

"Why do they love Jesus?"

"He died for their sins."

"Does everybody have sins?"

"Yes."

"Certainly you don't have any."

"One."

"What sin is that?"

"I make my mother angry."

"How do you make your mother angry, Pam?"

"I have trouble remembering to brush my teeth."

Beth

"Who's God, Beth?"

"He gives babies to people."

"I think that's very nice of Him."

Silence.

"Don't you think so?"

"I guess."

"Don't you like babies, Beth?"

"I guess."

"And don't you want to have some of your own some day?"

"I guess."

"You don't sound very happy about it."

"I am, but—"

"But what?"

Silence.

"Why aren't you happy about having babies some day, Beth?"

Silence.

"Won't you tell me?"

"Yes."

"Then what's worrying you so?"

"I just don't want God to give me any babies until I'm grown-up."

"When will that be, Beth?"

"When I'm in the fourth grade, I guess."

Janice

"Who's God, Janice?"

"Nobody."

"What do you mean, nobody?"

"Nobody."

"You don't believe in God?"

"No."

"Do you belive in Christ, Janice?"

"No."

"Have you ever heard of the Bible?"

"Yes."

"And the New Testament?"

"Yes."

"What are they?"

"Stories."

"Stories about what?"

"God and Christ."

"Does anyone ever read any of the stories to you?"

"My mother."

"Don't you learn a lot about God and Christ from them?"

"No."

"Why not?"

"I don't listen."

"Why don't you listen?"

"I don't want to hear them."

"Why don't you?"

"They're a lot of baloney."

"Baloney?"

"Yes."

"Who says they're baloney?"

"My father."

"Your father told you that?"

"No."

"Then how do you know he thinks they are?"

"I heard him tell my mother."

"What did your mother say?"

"She got mad."

"Does your mother go to church, Janice?"

"Yes."

"I take it that your father doesn't."

"He used to."

"With your mother?"

"No."

"Why not with your mother?"

"They belong to different churches."

"Why did your father stop going?"

"Because my mother goes all the time."

"All the time?"

"Every day. Lots of times twice a day."

"Do you go to church, Janice?"

"I have to."

"Have to?"

"My mother makes me."

"Everytime she goes?"

"Just on Sundays."

"Do you take part in the service, Janice?"

"No."

"You must hear what's going on."

"No."

"How can you help not hearing?"

"I shut my ears."

"How do you do that?"

"The same way as when my mother reads to me. I think hard about other things."

"You must *see* what's going on."

"No."

"How do you manage that?"

"I count the panes in the windows."

"Why don't you like church, Janice? Why don't you believe in God and Christ?"

Silence.

"Is it because your father doesn't?"

"No."

"Why then?"

Silence.

"Do you have a reason, Janice?"

"Yes."

"Then what is it?"

"My mother."

"Your mother?"

"Yes."

"Why is it your mother, Janice?"

"Because she loves God and Christ more than my father and me."

Larry

"Who's God, Larry?"

"The Creator."

"What's a creator?"

"Someone who makes things."

"What did God make, Larry?"

"The earth."

"What else?"

"Adam and Eve."

"Who were Adam and Eve?"

"The first people on earth."

"Are Adam and Eve the only people that God made?"

"Yes."

"Then where have all the millions of other people come from?"

"Adam and Eve."

"Do you mean that all the people on earth today are descendants of Adam and Eve?"

"Descendants?"

"Relatives."

Silence.

"Are all the people on earth today relatives of Adam and Eve, Larry?"

"Doesn't everyone know that?"

Ben

"Who's God, Ben?"

"A ghost."

"A ghost?"

"Yes."

"What kind of ghost?"

"Just a ghost."

"What does He look like?"

"You can't see Him."

"You mean He's invisible?"

"Yes."

"Why is He invisible?"

"All ghosts are."

"Why are they?"

"Because they're not real people."

"What are they?"

"Ghosts."

"Who told you that God is a ghost, Ben?"

"The minister."

"What minister?"

"The one in the church my mother and father take me to."

"What did the minister say?"

"That God is a ghost."

"He told you that?"

"Not just me."

"Who else?"

"Everybody in the audience."

"Exactly what did the minister say?"

"He called God the Ghost."

"That's all?"

"No."

"What else?"

"He called the Ghost by his first name."

"What is the Ghost's first name?"

"Holy."

"He called Him Holy Ghost?"

"Yes."

"More than once?"

"Every Sunday."

"What else does the minister say about Holy Ghost?"

"That He has a son."

"What's the son's name?"

"Jesus Christ."

"Is Jesus Christ a ghost, too?"

"No."

"What is He?"

"A real man."

"Like you and me?"

"Sort of."

"What do you mean by sort of?"

"He's dead."

"When did He die?"

"A few years ago."

"Why did He die?"

"He was bad."

"Jesus Christ was bad?"

"Yes."

"How do you know He was bad?"

"Because He was hung."

"Hung how?"

"On a cross."

"Who told you that Jesus Christ was bad, Ben?"

"The minister."

"The minister!"

"Yes."

"What did the minister say?"

"That Holy Ghost and all the people in the world are suffering for Jesus Christ's sins."

Helen

"Who's God, Helen?"

"My father."

"Your father?"

"Yes."

"Why do you think your father is God, Helen?"

"Because."

"Because what?"

"He's in Heaven."

"Your father is in Heaven?"

"Yes."

"I didn't know, Helen. I'm sorry."

"He was killed in the war."

"The Vietnam war?"

"I think so."

"And he went to Heaven and became God?"

"Yes."

"Are you sure he became God?"

"Yes."

"Why are you so sure, Helen?"

"It says so in the prayer my brother and I say every might before we go to bed."

"What prayer is that?"

"God's prayer."

"What does it say in the prayer about your father being God, Helen?"

"Our Father who art in Heaven."

"The Our Father in the prayer is your own Father?"

"Of course."

"And so he must be God?"

"Of course."

47

Jimmy

"Who's God, Jimmy?"
"I don't know."
"What's God like, Jimmy?"
"I don't know."
"Does anyone know?"
"Yes."
"Who?"
"The astronauts who went to the moon."
"The astronauts?"
"Yes."
"They know what God's like?"
"Yes."
"How?"
"They saw Him."
"Do you mean that God lives on the moon?"
"Yes."
"Did the astronauts discover that when they got there?"
"No."
"They knew beforehand?"
"Yes."

"And the reason they're all going to the moon is to see Him?"

"Yes."

"I wish you'd explain one thing to me, Jimmy. We've seen the astronauts and the moon on television. Why didn't we see God, too?"

"They didn't show pictures of God."

"But the astronauts must have taken some."

"They did."

"Has anyone seen the pictures?"

"Yes."

"Who?"

"The President."

"But no one else?"

"No."

"Why not, Jimmy?"

"It's secret information."

"Why is it secret?"

"I don't know."

"Who told you about all this, Jimmy?"

"My brother."

"Your brother's older than you, isn't he?"

"Yes."

"How much older?"

"Seven years."

"Do your mother and father know he told you about the astronauts seeing God?"

"No."

"What else has your brother told you about God?"

"He says God has angels flying around watching me."

"Watching you, why?"

"To see if I'm bad."

"What will the angels do if you're bad?"

"Take me to the moon."

"Why?"

"So God can punish me."

"Does your brother say how God will punish you?"

"Yes."

"How?"

"Burn me."

"Burn you?"

"Yes."

"How?"

"There's a cave in the moon with fire in it."

"And?"

"God has a mean angel who'll put me in it."

"Your brother told you that, Jimmy?"

"Yes."

"And you believe it?"

"Yes."

"Why do you believe it?"

"My brother showed me some pictures in a book."

"Of the cave and fire?"

"Yes."

"Tell me, Jimmy. Does your brother ever go to church?"

"Every Sunday."

"*Every* Sunday?"

"Yes."

"I didn't think he was religious."

"What does religious mean?"

"That he loves and worships God."

"Oh."

"Do you think your brother loves and worships God, Jimmy?"

"Of course."

"Why do you think so?"

"He sings in the choir."

"Why else do you think so?"

"Because he knows everything about God."

Louise

"Who's God, Louise?"

"There isn't any God."

"Who says there isn't?"

"My father and mother."

"Your father and mother told you that there isn't any God?"

"Sort of."

"Not actually?"

"No."

"How did they say it?"

"They stopped going to church."

"How else did they say there isn't any God?"

"They stopped taking me to Sunday school."

"How else?"

"They stopped saying grace before meals."

"How else?"

"They don't ever talk about God any more."

"You mean that they did believe in God once, but don't now?"

"Yes."

"When did this change happen, Louise?"

"A little while ago."

"What happened a little while ago?"

"My baby brother died."

"And that's when your mother and father turned against God?"

"Yes."

"Why?"

"They said it was God's fault."

"You heard them say that?"

"Yes."

"When?"

"When my brother died my mother cried all night."

"How do you know?"

"I sleep in the next room and heard her."

"What else did you hear?"

"My mother and father talking."

"What were they saying?"

"That God took my brother away."

"They were blaming Him?"

"Yes."

"Do *you* blame Him, Louise?"

"Yes."

"Because your mother and father do?"

Silence.

"Do you think your mother and father will always blame God, Louise?"

"Yes."

"And will you, too?"

"Yes."

Sally

"Who's God, Sally?"

"A millionaire?"

"Did you say a millionaire?"

"Yes."

"Do you know what a millionaire is, Sally?"

"Sure."

"What?"

"Someone with a lot of money."

"God has a lot of money?"

"Sure."

"How do you know He has?"

"Everyone knows that."

"How does everyone know?"

"Because when they go to church they have to pay admission."

"How much admission?"

"Five dollars."

"How do you know it's five dollars?"

"That's what my mother and father have to pay."

"How do they pay it, Sally?"

"The minister has people walk around the church with baskets and everyone puts money in them."

"And that money goes to God?"

"Yes."

"And that's why He's a millionaire?"

"Yes."

"What do you suppose God does with all that money, Sally?"

"Spends it."

"On what?"

"His house."

"Does He have a big house?"

"The biggest in Heaven."

"Who says so?"

"God."

"What does God say about it?"

"He calls it His mansion."

"And a mansion is a big house?"

"Yes."

"How do you know that?"

"I asked my father."

"Do you ever put money in the baskets, Sally?"

"Not in church."

"Where?"

"In Sunday school."

"You put money in the baskets in Sunday school?"

"No."

"What *do* you do?"

"We have a cardboard box."

"And you put the money in the box?"

"Yes."

"And then the money goes to God?"

"No."

"Where does it go?"

"To Jesus."

"Jesus?"

"That's God's son."

"And what does Jesus do with it?"

"Keeps it."

"How do you know Jesus keeps it?"

"It says so in the song."

"What song?"

"The song we sing when we put the money in the box."

"Is Jesus a millionaire, too, Sally?"

"No."

"Doesn't He have a mansion like God?"

"No."

"Why not?"

"He's poor."

"Poor?"

"He must be."

"Why must He be?"

"Because admission to get into Sunday school isn't as much as it is to go to church."

"How much is it to get into Sunday school, Sally?"

"It says in the song."

"What does the song say?"

"Do you want to hear it?"

"I'd like to very much, Sally."

"Hear the pennies dropping, dropping as they fall, every one for Jesus, He will get them all."

Joan

"Who's God, Joan?"

"Me."

"You're God?"

"Sort of."

"In what way are you sort of?"

"I'm like Him."

"Like Him?"

"I mean I was born like Him."

"How were you born like Him?"

"In His image."

"Where did you hear that?"

"I forget."

"What exactly did you hear?"

"That everybody's born in God's image."

"Do you know what image means?"

"My mother says it's what you see when you look in the mirror."

"When you look in the mirror what do you see?"

"Me."

"And, therefore, God?"

Silence.

"And God, Joan?"

"I couldn't."

"Why couldn't you?"

"Because He's a man, and I'm a girl."

"Well, if you don't look like God do you know in what other way you could be like Him?"

"No. I guess I'm a little mixed up."

"Not entirely, Joan. You were absolutely right when you said you were born in His image. All children are."

"They are?"

"Yes."

"How?"

"They're born with God's goodness in them."

Silence.

"They're born with His love in them."

Silence.

"And intelligence."

"What's that?"

"The ability to grow."

"How?"

"In wisdom."

Silence.

"In understanding."

Silence.

"In compassion."

Silence.

"Do you understand a little better now in what other way you were born in God's image, Joan?"

"Yes."

"You sound a little disappointed about it."

Silence.

"Why are you disappointed, Joan?"

"I wish I was, but I'm not *that* good."

Cliff

"Who's God, Cliff?"

"The Lord."

"That's right. God does have two names."

"He has more than just two."

"Oh?"

"Sure."

"How many does He have?"

Silence.

"Don't you know, Cliff?"

"I'm counting."

"His names?"

"Yes."

"How many do you count?"

"Four."

"God and the Lord are two. What are the other two?"

"Father."

"That's three. What's the fourth?"

"It says in His prayer. Hallowed. Hallowed be Thy name."

Ruthy

"Who's God, Ruthy?"

"My friend."

"Has He always been your friend?"

"Yes, but especially now."

"In what way is God your special friend now?"

"He's come to see me a lot lately."

"Here at the hospital?"

"Yes."

"When does He come to see you?"

"At night mostly."

"Why at night mostly?"

"Because He knows I'm loneliest then."

"Don't you sleep at night?"

"Not much."

"Doesn't the nurse give you anything to make you sleep?"

"Yes, but it doesn't last long."

"Can't you ask for more?"

"I guess so."

"Don't you?"

"No."

"Why not?"

"I don't need to."

"Why don't you need to?"

"Because when God's with me I don't hurt so much."

"Can you tell when God's with you?"

"Yes."

"How?"

"I can feel Him in the room with me."

"What do you do when He's with you?"

"I talk to Him."

"What about?"

"I tell Him everything that happened during the day."

"You mean like who's come to see you?"

"Nobody's allowed to come and see me except my mother and father and you."

"What else do you tell Him?"

"All the things the nurses and doctors have done to me."

"What else?"

"He listens to my prayers."

"You love God very much, don't you, Ruthy?"

"Yes."

"And you and God are very close, aren't you?"

"Yes."

"That must be a great comfort to you."

"I'm not afraid any more."

"Why not, Ruthy?"

"Because when I die and go to Heaven He'll be my friend there, too."

Harold

"Who's God, Harold?"

"The smartest person in the world."

"Smartest?"

"Yes."

"Smartest in what way, Harold?"

"He can do anything."

"What do you mean by anything?"

"Anything."

"For instance?"

"He can make anything."

"Like what?"

"Houses, and cars, and trains, and airplanes."

"He makes them himself?"

"No. He tells men how to make them."

"What else can God make?"

"Trees, and flowers, and grass."

"What else?"

"Birds, and animals, and fish, and people."

"You have great faith in God's abilities, don't you, Harold?"

"What does abilities mean?"

"Being able to make the things you mentioned."

"Yes."

"And you must love Him very much."

"No."

"You don't?"

"No."

"Why not?"

"Because."

"Because what?"

"I'm afraid of Him."

"Afraid?"

"Yes."

"Why should you be afraid of God?"

"Because He's so smart."

"You're afraid of His smartness?"

"Yes."

"Why?"

"Because He can unmake things, too."

"How can He unmake things like cars, and trains, and airplanes?"

"With accidents."

"And houses?"

"With fire."

"What about trees, and flowers, and grass?"

"With fire, too. Or without giving them any rain."

"How about birds, and animals, and fish?"

"He can make them get sick and die."

"And people?"

"He can make them die, too."

"Is that what you're afraid of? That God will make you die?"

"Yes."

"Why should you be afraid of that?"

"Mrs. Peterson."

"Who's Mrs. Peterson?"

"The lady down the street."

"What has she got to do with your being afraid of dying?"

"She said I was going to."

"She told you that?"

"Yes."

"Is that why you've been so nervous lately?"

Silence.

"What did Mrs. Peterson say to you, Harold?"

"That God would punish me."

"Punish you, why?"

"She said I was wicked."

"Were you?"

"Yes."

"What did you do that was wicked?"

"I had a fight with Joe Peterson."
"Is that her son?"
"Yes."
"What happened?"
"He kicked my dog."
"And what did you do?"
"I gave him a bloody nose."
"Is that what made Mrs. Peterson angry?"
"No."
"What else did you do?"
"Before I gave Joe a bloody nose I cursed him."
"What did you say?"
Silence.
"What, Harold?"
"Goddamn you."
"And Mrs. Peterson heard you?"
"No. Joe told her."
"And what did Mrs. Peterson say?"
"That God would strike me dead."

Ginny

"Who's God, Ginny?"

"God."

"What do you think He's like?"

"Sort of a guardian angel."

"Do you mean that He watches over you?"

"Yes."

"Just you?"

"No."

"Who else?"

"Lots of people."

"How do you know He watches over them, Ginny?"

"I ask Him to."

"How do you ask Him to?"

"In my prayer."

"What prayer is that?"

"Now I lay me down to sleep, I pray the Lord my soul to keep; if I should die before I wake, I pray the Lord my soul to take."

"Doesn't that prayer sound a little as though you were asking Him to watch over just you?"

"That's only part of the prayer."

"Excuse me. I didn't mean to interrupt."

"There's lots more."

"Do you want to tell it to me?"

"Yes."

"How does it go?"

"God bless Mother and Dad."

"Of course."

"And God bless my brother, Mike; and my sister, Sally."

"Of course."

"And God bless my grandmother and grandfather Kent; and my grandmother and grandfather Lane."

"Of course."

"And God bless my godmother, Mrs. Slaughter; and my godfather, Mr. Patterson."

"Good."

"And God bless Mary Lou."

"Who's Mary Lou?"

"The lady who comes in every week to clean our house."

"How else does your prayer go, Ginny?"

"God bless Aunt Mary and Uncle George."

"Go on."

"God bless Aunt Helen and Uncle Joe."

"Go on."

"God bless Miss Hatcher."

"Who's Miss Hatcher?"

"My kindergarten teacher."

"That's very nice."

"And God bless June, and Laura, and Pete."

"Who're they, Ginny?"

"My best friends."

"Are there any more?"

"Yes."

"Who?"

"God bless Mr. and Mrs. Lindsey."

"Who're Mr. and Mr. Lindsey?"

"Our neighbors on one side of us."

"Who else?"

"God bless Mr. and Mrs. Young."

"Are they your neighbors on the other side?"

"Yes."

"Anyone else?"

"God bless Mr. and Mrs. Stockler, and Mr. and Mrs. Wakefield."

"Who're they?"

"Our neighbors across the street."

"Is that all, Ginny?"

"No."

"Who else do you pray for?"

"Old Dave."

"Who's Old Dave?"

"Our yard man."

"Go on."

"God bless Cindy."

"Who's Cindy?"

"Our dog."

"And?"

"And God bless Patches."

"Your cat?"

"Yes."

"Are there any more, Ginny?"

"No."

"That's all?"

"Yes."

"It's quite a long list. Do you pray for them all every night?"

"Yes."

"Why?"

"I'm afraid something might happen to them if I didn't."

"What do you suppose would happen to them if you didn't?"

"God might not watch over their souls."

"Do you know what the soul is, Ginny?"

"Sure."

"What is it?"

"Can I tell you some other time?"

"Why some other time, Ginny?"

"I've got to go out now and play."

Alex

"Who's God, Alex?"

"Which one?"

"Is there more than one God?"

"Of course."

"How many Gods are there?"

"I've never tried to count them all."

"How many would you guess?"

"Hundreds."

"Hundreds?"

"Yes."

"Why are there so many Gods, Alex?"

"There has to be."

"Why does there have to be?"

"Because there're hundreds of Heavens."

"There are?"

"Sure."

"And each one has a different God?"

"Yes."

"What's one of the Heavens, Alex?"

"The one I'm going to."

"Just you?"

"No."

"Who else?"

"Everybody who lives in America."

"And this Heaven has the God we go to church to worship?"

"Yes."

"What other Heaven is there, Alex?"

"The China Heaven."

"And it has a Chinese God?"

"Yes."

"What other Heavens are there?"

"The England Heaven. The Italy Heaven. The India Heaven. The Russia Heaven."

"You certainly know a lot about the different countries in the world, Alex."

"I like to look at maps and geography books."

"And the people who live in all the countries on the maps and in the geography books have a different Heaven and a different God?"

"Yes."

"That does make for quite a few Heavens."

"Those're only part of the Heavens."

"There're others?"

"Sure."

"What others?"

"The animal Heavens."

"The animal Heavens?"

"Yes."

"Do you mean that animals have their own Heavens?"

"Yes."

"There's a dog Heaven?"

"Yes."

"And a cat Heaven?"

"Yes."

"And a horse Heaven?"

"Yes."

"What about the Gods in these Heavens? Are they animal Gods?"

"Of course."

"Why are there so many Heavens and Gods, Alex?"

"There has to be."

"Why does there have to be?"

"Because."

"Because what?"

"There isn't room in just one for all the people and animals who die."

Tom

"Who's God, Tom?"

"The greatest."

"In what way is God the greatest?"

"He sent His son down to earth."

"Do you mean Jesus?"

"Yes."

"Why did God send Jesus down to earth?"

"To do miracles."

"What kind of miracles did Jesus do?"

"He walked on water."

"What other miracles?"

"He had some loaves of bread and some fish and he made them into thousands so the poor people wouldn't go hungry."

"What other miracles?"

"He made sick people well."

"Were there any more?"

"He ascended."

"What do you mean by ascend?"

"Fly?"

"Jesus was able to fly?"

"He must have been."

"Where did Jesus fly, Tom?"

"Heaven."

"Why Heaven?"

"To be with His father again."

Nancy

"Who's God, Nancy?"

"I don't know exactly."

"Does anyone know exactly?"

"No."

"What do you think God's like, Nancy?"

"A spirit."

"What kind of a spirit?"

"One that's everywhere."

"God's everywhere?"

"Yes."

"What does He do?"

"Everything."

"Can you give me an example?"

"He runs the world."

"In what way?"

"He makes it work."

"How?"

"He makes it go around."

"How else does He make the world work?"

"He makes it rain and snow."

"How else?"

"He makes things grow."

"What things?"

"Birds, fish, animals, trees, flowers."

"What else?"

"People."

"Everything you've told me about God are good things, aren't they?"

"Yes."

"Does He ever do bad things?"

"No."

"Nothing?"

"No."

"What about making things die?"

"That's not really bad."

"It isn't?"

"No."

"Why isn't it?"

"Because He never makes things—or people—die forever."

"You believe in eternal life then?"

"Yes."

"Do you know what is meant by eternal life?"

"People don't die forever."

"How do you know about it?"

"My father told me."

"Has your father told you a lot about God?"

"Yes."

"What's the most important thing he's told you?"

"About eternal life."

"Why is it important to you?"

"Because when I die I'll be able to be with my mother again."

"I'm sorry, Nancy. I didn't know your mother was dead."

"She isn't."

"She isn't?"

"She's just dead here on earth."

"But alive somewhere else?"

"Yes."

"Where?"

"In Heaven, naturally."

"Everyone who goes to Heaven is alive?"

"Of course."

"It's a very wonderful and a very comforting thing to have faith as strong as yours."

"It isn't faith."

"It isn't?"

"No."

"What is it, Nancy?"

"The truth. I am going to be with my mother again. I am! I just know I am!"

Kent

"Who's God, Kent?"

"Jesus' father in Heaven."

"If God lives in Heaven why wasn't Jesus born in Heaven?"

"Because His mother lived on earth."

"Why did God want Jesus to be born on earth?"

"So when He grew up Jesus could preach on earth."

"What did Jesus preach on earth?"

"Lots of things."

"Do you believe in what Jesus preached, Kent?"

"I do now."

"Why now?"

"Because sometimes when I didn't, I got into trouble."

"With your parents?"

"No."

"With your teacher?"

"No."

"With whom, Kent?"

"My conscience."

"What's your conscience, Kent?"

"A voice that guides me."

"Who's God, Jill?"

"Love."

"In what way is God love?"

"He loves everybody."

"In what other way is God love?"

"Everybody loves *Him.*"

"Is there another way?"

"Because of Him everybody in the world loves everybody else."

"Do you love everybody else in the world?"

"Yes."

"And does everybody in the world love you?"

"Yes."

"Don't you ever get a little bit mad at anybody?"

"Sometimes."

"When you're mad at them don't you stop loving them?"

"No."

"Not even for a little while?"

"No."

"Why not?"

"I can't."

"Why can't you?"

"My Sunday school teacher says that God is in me."

"And because God is love and in you, you love people even when you're mad at them?"

"That's not the only reason."

"What other reason is there?"

"My Sunday school teacher says that God is in everyone."

"Go on."

"Well, if I ever stopped loving anyone I'd stop loving God, and I couldn't ever do that."